LANDSCAPES OF LIVING & DYING

Selected Works by Lawrence Ferlinghetti

POETRY

Pictures of the Gone World (City Lights Books, 1955)
A Coney Island of the Mind (New Directions, 1958)
Translation: Jacques Prévert, *Paroles*
(City Lights Books, 1958)
Starting from San Francisco (New Directions, 1967)
The Secret Meaning of Things (New Directions, 1968)
Back Roads to Far Places (New Directions, 1971)
Open Eye, Open Heart (New Directions, 1973)
Who Are We Now? (New Directions, 1976)
Landscapes of Living & Dying (New Directions, 1979)

PROSE

Her (New Directions, 1960)
Tyrannus Nix? (New Directions, 1969)
The Mexican Night (New Directions, 1970)

PLAYS

Unfair Arguments with Existence (New Directions, 1963)
Routines (New Directions, 1964)

FILMS

Have You Sold Your Dozen Roses? (1960)
Tyrannus Nix? (N.E.T., 1969)
Assassination Raga, with Max Crosley (1973)

RECORDINGS

Poetry Readings in "The Cellar," with Kenneth Roxroth
(Fantasy LP7002, 1958)
*Tentative Description of a Dinner to Impeach
President Eisenhower & Other Poems* (Fantasy LP7004, 1959)
The World's Great Poets, Volume I, with Allen Ginsberg
and Gregory Corso, Spoleto Festival, 1965
(CMS LP617, 1971)
Tyrannus Nix? & Assassination Raga (Fantasy LP7014, 1971)

LAWRENCE FERLINGHETTI

LANDSCAPES
OF
LIVING
&
DYING

A NEW DIRECTIONS BOOK

Manufactured in the United States of America
First published clothbound in 1979, as New Directions Paperbook 491, and in a signed, limited edition
Published simultaneously in Canada by George J. McLeod, Ltd., Toronto

Library of Congress Cataloging in Publication Data
Ferlinghetti, Lawrence.
    Landscapes of living & dying.
    (A New Directions Book)
    I. Title.
PS3511.E557L3   811'.5'4   79-15595
ISBN 0-8112-0741-2
ISBN 0-8112-0743-9 limited ed.
ISBN 0-8112-0742-0 pbk.

New Directions Books are published for James Laughlin
by New Directions Publishing Corporation,
80 Eighth Avenue, New York 10011

CONTENTS

THE OLD ITALIANS DYING

For years the old Italians have been dying
all over America
For years the old Italians in faded felt hats
have been sunning themselves and dying
You have seen them on the benches
in the park in Washington Square
the old Italians in their black high button shoes
the old men in their old felt fedoras
       with stained hatbands
have been dying and dying
        day by day

You have seen them
every day in Washington Square San Francisco
the slow bell
tolls in the morning
in the Church of Peter & Paul
in the marzipan church on the plaza
toward ten in the morning the slow bell tolls
in the towers of Peter & Paul
and the old men who are still alive
sit sunning themselves in a row
on the wood benches in the park
and watch the processions in an out
funerals in the morning
weddings in the afternoon
slow bell in the morning Fast bell at noon
In one door out the other
the old men sit there in their hats
and watch the coming & going
You have seen them
the ones who feed the pigeons
     cutting the stale bread
       with their thumbs & penknives

the ones with old pocketwatches
the old ones with gnarled hands
                    and wild eyebrows
the ones with the baggy pants
                    with both belt & suspenders
the grappa drinkers with teeth like corn
the Piemontesi the Genovesi the Sicilianos
                    smelling of garlic & pepperonis
the ones who loved Mussolini
the old fascists
the ones who loved Garibaldi
the old anarchists reading *L'Umanita Nova*
the ones who loved Sacco & Vanzetti
They are almost all gone now
They are sitting and waiting their turn
and sunning themselves in front of the church
over the doors of which is inscribed
a phrase which would seem to be unfinished
from Dante's *Paradiso*
about the glory of the One
                    who moves everything . . .
The old men are waiting
for it to be finished
for their glorious sentence on earth
                    to be finished
the slow bell tolls & tolls
the pigeons strut about
not even thinking of flying
the air too heavy with heavy tolling
The black hired hearses draw up
the black limousines with black windowshades
shielding the widows
the widows with the long black veils
who will outlive them all
You have seen them

2

madre di terra, madre di mare
The widows climb out of the limousines
The family mourners step out in stiff suits
The widows walk so slowly
up the steps of the cathedral
fishnet veils drawn down
leaning hard on darkcloth arms
Their faces do not fall apart
They are merely drawn apart
They are still the matriarchs
outliving everyone
the old dagos dying out
in Little Italys all over America
the old dead dagos
hauled out in the morning sun
that does not mourn for anyone
One by one Year by year
they are carried out
The bell
never stops tolling
The old Italians with lapstrake faces
are hauled out of the hearses
by the paid pallbearers
in mafioso mourning coats & dark glasses
The old dead men are hauled out
in their black coffins like small skiffs
They enter the true church
for the first time in many years
in these carved black boats
                    ready to be ferried over
The priests scurry about
                as if to cast off the lines
The other old men
                    still alive on the benches
watch it all with their hats on

You have seen them sitting there
waiting for the bocci ball to stop rolling
waiting for the bell
                    to stop tolling & tolling
for the slow bell
                    to be finished tolling
telling the unfinished *Paradiso* story
as seen in an unfinished phrase
                    on the face of a church
as seen in a fisherman's face
in a black boat without sails
making his final haul

THE SEA AND OURSELVES
AT CAPE ANN

Caw Caw Caw
on a far shingle long ago
when as a boy I came here
put ear to shell
        of the thundering sea
            sundering sea
     seagulls high over
        calling & calling
      back then
        at Cape Ann Gloucester
Where Olson saw himself Ishmael
  and wrote his own epitaph:
        'I set out now
         in a box upon the sea'
And Creeley found his creel
      yet would not / cd. not
        speak of the sea
And Ferrini took the wind's clothes
   and became the conscience of Gloucester
Yet none could breathe
        a soul into the sea
And I saw the tide pools gasping
  the sea's mouth roaring
        polyphoboistrous
    beyond the Ten Pound Light
       roistering
        off far islands
   'Les Trois Sauvages'
Where Eliot heard
     the sea's stark meditation
  off *beauport* Gloucester

Where I as a man much later
                made a landfall in the gloaming
        sighting from seaward in convoy
                    beyond the gulls' far off
                                tattered cries
                cats' cries lost
                    reached to us
                        in shredded snatches
        Then as now
Eliot must
            have been a seaman
                            in his city-soul
        to have heard so deeply
                the sea's voice sounding then
                    in 'The Dry Salvages'
Here now
        where now
                    is the sea's urge still
        sea's surge and thunder
                        except within us
                    folded under
        by the beach road now
                        rapt in darkness
The sea still a great door never opened
        great ships asunder
                    clinker-built bottoms
            nets hung with cork
                    hulls heavy with caulking
While still the Nor'easter blows
            still the high tides
                seethe & sweep shoreward
        batter the breakwaters
                the granite harbors
                        rock villages
        Land's End lashed again
                    in 'the sudden fury'

And still the stoned gulls soaring over
                crying & calling & crying
     blissed-out up there
              in the darkening air
    over the running sea
            the runing sea
    over dark stone beach under stars
Where now we sit
       'distracted from distraction' still
   Odyssey turned to *Iliad*
          in parked cars

THE MAJESTY

The majesty the sad majesty

        of the universe

                on grey mornings

the clouds the furled clouds the grey seas

    like sheets of iron

          Sails on them

      like rusty tin tongues

             struck silent

vaults of sky shut up

        on huge hinges

    keys thrown away

           into Turner landscapes

'Face of creation' veiled unsmiling

    the waves are mute lips

          curled back

Silence and no answer

        in any 'objective correlative'

    or 'pathetic fallacy'

          The fog

            finds the dumb bell

A dog looks out a port

        daring not to bark

          and tear the veil today

THE PIED PIPER OF IRON MOUNTAIN

The plane drones toward Iron Mountain Michigan
The sun is setting The seatbelt sign comes on
It is a red dusk We are circling lower
The plane groans as its wheels are lowered
There is a distant rumbling
It is the Iron Mountain opening
On huge sliding hinges
          the side of the mountain
                    is sliding open
                         with a deep rumbling
The plane is roaring right toward it
I can see its shadow fleeing along the ground
The yawning minehead
                    sticks out its black tongue
Smoke pours out
                    The roaring grows louder
A small narrow-gauge track
          sticks out the mouth like a bent straw
                    disgorging a line of iron-ore cars
Close to the ground now
          our plane lumbers along
                    bumping the hot air
I can see huge mills behind us
          great fires glowing red
                    blind stacks belching smoke
     blear factories stretched out
                         over the plains
                    the forges glowing red
                         Dark satanic mills!
I look back and see
          myriad trucks and cars
                    on the asphalt ground
          all roaring along after us

I take out a small flute
I look down and see myself
I am dressed in a sharp business suit
I have a plastic name-plate on my lapel
I have short hair
                    and a pocketful of credit cards
I am clean-shaved with a slight paunch
I have a plastic highball in my hand
My wife is at home with the kiddies
                    in the suburbs of Pittsburgh
I have steely blue eyes and a digital wristwatch
I put the flute to my lips and blow
I look back and see
                    all our iron progeny
                            following me
                riding planes and trucks and trains and cars
The horizon behind us
                        is blackened with them
Their smoke obscures the last light
                    It may be the year two thousand
Now close ahead
            the black mouth of Iron Mountain
                        shudders to receive us
                            with a great gnashing
We zoom straight
                    through the hot iron gates
The whole bright horde of our children
                            roars in after us
And the gates of Iron Mountain
                            clang shut

There once was a garden called Earth

Outside in the night
            on the slopes of Iron Mountain
                    a great silence descends

11

The sky cleans itself
        and the stars come out
                in the total darkness

It is one of those so clear nights
        out on the plains of America
            when the big sky seems so close
                you can touch the stars
It is so quiet
        you can hear
            the new grass growing

A NATION OF SHEEP

Flying over the snowfields
of northern Wisconsin
flying low through the Harrisburg fallout
in a twin-engine Cessna
I look down and see
meek cows in the snow
attached to Moo-matic milking machines
tended by Alices in Dairyland
and huge hogs and huge steer
hooked into 'Hot Dog Highways'
producing 36,000 wieners per hour
The beast is fed in by the head
and comes out a dead dog
tongue-tied
The pigs and cows and steer
are all snowed under
as the people are snowed under
by the white rain of laundered news
from government laundries
at Three Mile Island
or wherever the white death breeds
The sky is filled with flocks of sheep
I look down and see the big snow
blanketing the great plains the far prairies
cities lost in it
Perhaps it's Siberia snowed under
with its hydroelectric plant at Zima
But this is not hydro
Here it's ceiling zero
as the snow flies
as Pluto flies
through the skies made of white sheep

Even in Siberia they don't have
such complete snowjobs
The little Cessna flies low
over the socked-in snowfields
It's a late spring silent spring
Flying low I see the fine print
the way you can't see it from high altitudes
on the big official carriers
I look down and see the fine grass roots
the people and cows and pigs
rooting and rutting and dying
feeding and breeding—
Dumb beasts all!
Dumb sheep snowblind
in the white zero snow
the hard white rain
that launders the sky
and falls and falls on the whitened grass
which the cows and pigs and people are eating
as if it were pure light
Even here in Middle America in Middle Earth
even though they know a snowjob when they see one
in the wilds of Wisconsin
or wherever the hard rain falls
they go on swallowing the snow-white lies
following each other head-to-tail
to the dim plutonium shores

*

Still in places not snowbound
in Middle America or Middle Earth
or wherever the hard rain falls

some students some long-hairs some Socratic grey-hairs
still alive in heart and head
are not being snowed
I see them walking with candles
up State Streets to capitols
I see their candles flickering
against the white night
flickering up capitol steps
to the chambers of power wherever
like fireflies everywhere
their candle power everywhere
upon the darkling plain

(An earlier version of this poem was read by the author and broadcast continuously by an FM station in Madison, Wisconsin, causing candlelight marches and vigils by students at the state capitol during the first week in April 1979.)

THE LOVE NUT

I go into the men's room Springfield bus station
on the way back to Muhlenberg County
and see this nut in the mirror
Who let in this weirdo Who let in this creep?
He's the kind writes I LOVE YOU on toilet walls and wants to
    embrace everybody in the lobby He writes his phone number
    inside a heart on the wall He's some kinda pervert Mister
    Eros the Great Lover
He wants to run up to everybody in the waiting room and kiss
    them on the spot and say Why aren't we friends and lovers
    Can I go home with you You got anything to drink or smoke
    Let's you and me get together The time is now or sooner
He wants to take all the stray dogs and cats and people home
    with him and turn them on to making love all the time
    wherever
He wants to scatter poems from airplanes across the landscape
    He's some kinda poetic nut Like he thinks he's Dylan
    Thomas and Bob Dylan rolled together with Charlie Chap-
    lin thrown in
He wants to lip-read everybody's thoughts and feelings and
    longings He's a dangerous nut He's gotta be insane He has
    no sense of sin
He wants to heat up all the dead-looking people the unhappy-
    looking people in bus stations and airports He wants to heat
    up their beds He wants to open their bodies and heads
He's some kinda airhead rolling stone He don't wanna be alone
    He may be queer on men
He's the kind addresses everybody on buses making them laugh
    and look away and then look back again

He wants to get everyone to burst out laughing and sighing and crying and singing and dancing and kissing each other including old ladies and policemen

He's gotta be mad He's so glad to be alive he's real strange He's got the hots for humanity one at a time He wants to kiss your breasts He wants to lie still between them singing in a low voice

He wants everyone to lie down together and roll around together moaning and singing and having visions and orgasms He wants to come in you He wants you to come with him He wants us all to come together One hot world One heartbeat

He wants he wants us all to lie down together in Paradise in the Garden of Love in the Garden of Delights and couple together like a train a chain-reaction a chain-letter-of-love around the world on hot nights

He wants he wants he wants! He's gotta be crazy Call the cops Take him away!

HOLIDAY INN BLUES

In a dark cave called Fuzzy's
             Holiday Inn Spartanburg South Carolina
    some weird ritual being performed
                     by the natives
           a sign proclaiming
     'Come Dance the Fuzz Off Your Peaches!'
a country-rock group working out
  an Elvis Presley singer
             bellows at four dim couples dancing
      two of them doing rock-style   .
                                not touching
                         or looking
                           at each other
             as they thrash about
           as if each were trying
                    to keep his or her balance
        on some erratic highspeed treadmill
The other two couples
                       wrapped around each other
             in the local bear-hug style

When the number is over
                       the dejected-looking couples
         wend their way back to their tables
Two of the men in lumberjack shirts
             shovel the ladies into their seats
        and retreat to their own tables

And the primitive rites continue
                    as two other locals sidle up
      and ask the same middle-age ladies to prance
  as I sit there making up fantastic fictional histories

        of these two made-up ladies in fancy hair-dos &
              doubleknit pants suits
One
    I imagine
             has three grown children in Greenville
          and a fat husband who travels
She has her hair done once a week
              by a lady barber from Asheville
        who specializes in blue hair & blue gossip
At her last blue appointment
            she learned her hubby had been
            running around with a
               gay hosiery salesman
                   in Atlanta
The other lady
          has never been married but
               for many years
   has been a receptionist
             for an elderly dentist
   and has been rumored to have always been
      quite receptive to the dentist
        whenever he said Open Wide

The cave dance comes to an end again
    and the two ladies slump back to their seats again
      and two more worthies in plaid shirts
        press themselves upon them
          and they're caught again
              in the bear-hug clutch
         the men hanging onto them
        as if they were
           absolutely starved for affection
      on a life-raft somewhere
        clinging to them like life itself
              or their mothers

     yet they are absolute strangers
        returning the ladies to their tables again
    with bows and 'thankya m'ams'

The bandleader makes some banter
    about 'them beautiful heffers' he seen on dancefloors
The cave ritual goes on
      as other younger couples struggle up
           and grapple with each other
  as the raunchy singer starts his Buddy Holly numbers
    Three electric guitars with red lights on them
       heat up behind him
      The cave lights glow redder and redder
           the couples more agitated
            emitting a desperate heat
      The electric fenders clash together
           with showers of sparks
      The drummer speeds up his freight train
      The loudspeakers smoke
           the whole cave rocks
  the writhing couples fall to the floor
     and roll upon each other
        with small passionate cries
     lips clinging to each other
        like suction cups
We've fallen into
      Dante's Inferno
        burning for love
We're trapped inside
      Bosch's Garden of Delights
        groaning with love
We're lost
    in Burroughs' loveless Soft Machine
       with tongues alack
         for love

CLONING AT THE 'HAWK & DOVE'

I wander into the "Hawk & Dove'
direct from the Library of Congress
Some super-guys and very-together-ladies
                                    at the bar
At the next table I hear a man
                        with a government voice
authoritatively announce to his visitor
that Washington DC is known for one thing
                            the bacon-cheeseburger
Here I'd thought DC was known
      as a seat of some imperial government
Two clones come in
                        circle about and land
                            on the other side of me
            both blond California golden boys
                        with hair in their eyes
One says 'I'm starved, man'
            the other 'I'm super-starved!'
They order bacon-cheeseburgers
                        One adds 'Or whatever'
The other pulls out a brochure
                        'Welcome to Washington'
            and stares at it
I am wishing for Ben Shahn's right-angle lens
                  to study their expressions
                        without freaking them out
John Denver comes on the jukebox singing
                        'I'm not half the man
                            I used to be'
One half of a clone or whatever
                        shakes his golden locks
                            off his beardless face
            and catches me
                  eyeballing him

like I'm Priapus
           spying on
                  a fertility rite
And I may be born again
my hair turned long and golden
                   a surfboard growing
                       from my feet
And I don't any longer feel
              'like Conrad carrying
                  Coleridge's albatross'

(*The final quotation is taken from Jill Johnston's description of the author in* The Village Voice.)

THE END OF VARIOUS AFFAIRS

What is that great crow doing
                    flying into my picture
        flying into my various love affairs
                        (with various 'Lenores')
            as if to mark the end
                            of my amores?
This huge black crow floats through
                            the salty air
        and lands on a branch by my window
                    stretching and shaking
                        its dingbat wings
The broken sky above the trees
    has birds for fishes
        in its seas
                    (What waves what rocks what shores!)
While this landlubber crow lets out
                        a great lost cry
            as if to mock the end
                        of my amore
        and louder and louder cries and cries
                        Never never nevermore!

A SWEET FLYING DREAM

We were two naked
                light-headed dandelions
                                with natural hair blown out
            floating high over the landscape
                            blown by zephyr winds
            our long legs dangling
                                    straight down
                        translucent
                                    dandelion stems
            in an archetypal primordial dream
                                    of flying
Sweet hills & waters
                    flowed below us
            as we floated high over
                            lakes & rivers
                                    & windblown peaks
We
    drifted
            wafted easily
                            We
                                flew wingless
        Full of air
                    our hair
                            buoyed us
    We
        trailed our slim legs
                            in streams of silver air
                    There
                            was nothing
                                    blowing us down
                                or away
                                        from each other

After a long way
              and a long while
                        we
                             glided down
                   lower & lower
         in great swinging circles
              The sea
                   the lapping sea
                             rose up
       and we
              were over
                   dry gold land
                             close up
     and I
         I was afraid you would
                   come against the ground too hard
         and I reached down
                   and took
                        your two extended hands
                             in mine
         and held you below me
                        like that
                             floating
As we drifted
         lower & lower
       the earth
              came up to us
                        so softly
     And   .
         we landed
                   so quietly
              sank
              so gently
                        to the bright soft ground
And lay in the light
                   flowerless fields

TWO SCAVENGERS IN A TRUCK,
TWO BEAUTIFUL PEOPLE IN A
MERCEDES

At the stoplight waiting for the light
                                  Nine A.M. downtown San Francisco
    a bright yellow garbage truck
                with two garbagemen in red plastic blazers
    standing on the back stoop
                    one on each side hanging on
      and looking down into
                    an elegant open Mercedes
        with an elegant couple in it
The man
        in a hip three-piece linen suit
           with shoulder-length blond hair & sunglasses
The young blond woman so casually coifed
               with a short skirt and colored stockings
    on the way to his architect's office

And the two scavengers up since Four A.M.
                        grungy from their route
        on the way home
The older of the two with grey iron hair
                   and hunched back
      looking down like some
                  gargoyle Quasimodo
And the younger of the two
                also with sunglasses & longhair
    about the same age as the Mercedes driver

And both scavengers gazing down
                as from a great distance
      at the cool couple

as if they were watching some odorless TV ad
            in which everything is always possible

And the very red light for an instant
            holding all four close together
      as if anything at all were possible
                        between them
      across that great gulf
                  in the high seas
                        of this democracy

THE BILLBOARD PAINTERS

The two
           white-overalled white-capped
                                          signpainters
                      on the high
                                 scaffold suspended
                      on the huge
                                billboard
                                beside the elevated
                                                   freeway
             painting a snapshot landscape of
                            a South Sea island beach
                   with lagoon and coral reef and
                                                 palmtrees
                           thru which the sun
                                         is setting and
the two
          white painters painting a
                                   sunburned
                           North American couple on the
                                                      white beach
           and the real sun cold
                   over the myriad flashing cars in
                        the middle of San Francisco
                   next to the Hall of questionmark
                                                Justice and
the two
          all-white painters
                                struck motionless with
                   arms and paintbrushes raised
                                     halfway thru the
                                        landscape with
                      the right half painted and

                    the left half still blank
                         white on white as if
                              the other half of the world had
                              still to be provided for
                              or as if
                                        God or some other
                    slightly less omnipotent
                                        Creator was maybe
                         changing his or her mind half-
                                   way thru as if
               even he or she was
                              not so certain anymore it
                              was such a good idea after
                                   all
                                        to have
these two so-white All American
                                   painters painting
          that paradise on earth
                              as if
               the advertisers who
                              were paying for this sign
               hadn't already recycled that
                                        particular paradise
          with a jet strip and
                              hotels looking like the
               American
                              roman empire where
               they had to advertise now in
                         order to fill those fancy
                              wateringplaces with
                                        retired billboard
                                        painters who
               belonged to the union and
                    got themselves and their wives
                    all these
                              benefits like

South Sea island trips after
working all their lives in
untropical places like
San Francisco
which

Sir Francis Drake found and
wrote back to the head of *his*
empire saying he
had just discovered
a real unspoiled
native paradise and
if they hurried and
put up billboards back home they
might just be able to
set up a colony out
here with
swimming pools and even maybe make
a pot of gold or
a killing and
die happy in
a beach chair
very far
from home

HOME HOME HOME

Where are they going
all these brave intrepid animals
Fur and flesh
in steel cabinets
on wheels
high-tailing it
Four PM Friday freeway
over the hidden land
San Francisco's burning
with the late sun
in a million windows
The four-wheeled animals
are leaving it to burn
They're escaping
almost flying
home to the nest
home to the warm caves
in the hidden hills & valleys
home to daddy home to mama
home to the little wonders
home to the pot plants behind the garage
The cars the painted cabinets
streak for home home home
THRU TRAFFIC MERGE LEFT
home to the hidden turning
the hidden yearning
home to San Jose
home to Santa Cruz & Monterey
home to Hamilton Avenue
home to the Safeway the safest way
YIELD
LEFT LANE MUST TURN LEFT

home to the little grey home in the West
home to Granddaddy on the golfcourse
home to Uncle Ned
puttering in the toolshed
having lost his pants
on the stock exchange
home to big sister
who lost her way in encounter groups
home to the 97-1b housewife
driving two tons of chrome & steel
three blocks to the supermarket
to buy a package of baby pins
home to little sister
blushing with boyfriends
in the laundryroom
home to kid brother with skateboards & Adidas
home to mad Uncle building CB radios
in hidden bunkers
home to backyard barbecues
with aerospace neighbors
Mr. Wilson's coming over
The Hendersons will all be there
Home to Hidden Valley
where the widow waits
by the Cross on the mountain
where hangs the true madness
home to Santa's Village
WILL DIVIDE TO SUIT
GAS FOOD LODGING NEXT RIGHT
home to where the food is
home to Watsonville
home to Salinas
past the Grapes of Wrath
past United Farmworkers

stooped over artichokes
home home over the horizon
where the sun still blows
into the sea
home to Big Sur
and the garden of delights
and the oranges of Hieronymous Bosch
the sun still sets
in lavender skies
Home sweet home the salesman sighs
home safe at home in the bathroom
safe with the washingmachine & dishwasher
safe with the waterheater
safe with the kitchen clock
tick tick
the time is not yet
the alarm is set
safe at last in the double bed
hidden from each other
in the dark bed by the winding stair
the enchanted place in the still air
hidden each from each
or the queensize bed the kingsize bed
the waterbed with the vibrator
with the nylon nympho in it
the bed of roses
the bed with Big Emma in it
with the stoned-out Angel in it
(Mountains of flesh
Hills of hips & thighs
Rolling landscapes of heaving meat
Groans & moans & cries!)
Home to the bed we made
and must lie in

with 'whoever'
Or home to the bed still to be made
of ragas & visions
the bed whose form is pure light
(and unheard melodies
dark despairs & inchoate ecstasies
longings out of reach)
Who to decipher them who answer them
singing each to each?
Hidden from themselves
The beds are warm with them
The springs quake
on the San Andreas Fault
The dark land broods
Look in my eye, look in my eye
the cyclope tv cries
It blinks and rolls its glassy eye
and shakes its vacuum head
over the shaken bodies
in the bed

SAN JOSE SYMPHONY RECEPTION

(*Flagrante delicto*)

The bald man in plaid playing the harpsichord
    stopped short and sidled over
                        to the sideboard
    and copped a piece of Moka
                       on a silver plate
    and slid back and started playing again
        some kind of Hungarian rhapsodate
    while the lady with the green eyeshades
        leaned over him exuding
                       admiration & lust
Half notes danced & tumbled
                   out of his instrument
    exuding a faint odor of
                 chocolate cake
In the corner I was taking
        a course in musical destruction
  from the dark lady cellist
    who bent over me with her bow unsheathed
    and proceeded to saw me in half
As a consequence my pants fell right off
    revealing a badly bent trombone which
        even the first flutist
           who had perfect embouchure
                 couldn't straighten out

WHITE ON WHITE

Today I'll write white on white
wear nothing but white
drink nothing but white
eat nothing but white
And I would be that sea-creature
who eats light
straining the ocean for its phosphorous—
For present time
is a 'white dot' in space
and white is the sand
in the hourglass
running out
White dunes of Africa
running through it
Snows of Siberia
sifting through it
The seas white with sperm
under the white moon
where aluminum stars wheel about
noiselessly
over quivering earth
with its white whales
white phagocytes
white bleached skulls
and albino animals
(Blacks bleached out
into white men?)
And to dream of white string
a symbol of innocence
Though the color of death be white
And the world checkered with death
white-on-black & black-on-white

'dumb pawns
in black-and-white kingdoms'
An angel stands on a station platform
slowly shaking its gossamer wings
A white horse
comes alone from a torn village
Everywhere around the earth
on station platforms they
are still putting up the placards
No pasaran
Go back Wrong way
White searchlights
search the sky
The gun turrets turn
on the old Walls
The angel slowly moves its wings
breathing the light white air
The earth breathes and trembles with it
The governed
will be governed
Liberty is not freedom
Eros versus civilization
No Way
without a pass
It is snowing white documents
The very rich
get richer still
A white gloved hand
still reaches out the window
for the money in the cup
Liberty is not free
The angel
stands on the edge
of the station platform

slowly moving its large white wings
which look too fragile
to lift the body of being
which still breathes anarchist air
And the train
the train made of nothing but boxcars
jammed with three billion people
still stands in the station trembling
And white phoenixes arise
out of piñon smoke
And the 'white sphinx of chance'
still holds its tongue
on the desert roads of the future

AN ELEGY TO DISPEL GLOOM

(After the assassinations of Mayor George Moscone and Supervisor Harvey Milk in San Francisco, November, 1978)

Let us not sit upon the ground
and tell sad stories
of the death of sanity.
That two sweet men are dead
is all that need be said.
Two such sentient beings
two humans made of flesh
are meshed in death
and no more need be said.
It is pure vanity
to think that all humanity
be bathed in red
because one young mad man
one so bad man
lost his head.
The force that through the red fuze
drove the bullet
does not drive everyone
through the City of Saint Francis
where there's a breathless hush
in the air today
a hush at City Hall
and a hush at the Hall of Justice
a hush in Saint Francis Wood
where no bird
tries to sing
a hush on the Great Highway
and in the great harbor
upon the great ships

and on the Embarcadero
from the Mission Rock Resort
to the Eagle Cafe
a hush on the great red bridge
and on the great grey bridge
a hush in the Outer Mission
and at Hunter's Point
a hush at a hot potato stand on Pier 39
and a hush at the People's Temple
where no bird
tries its wings
a hush and a weeping
at the Convent of the Sacred Heart
on Upper Broadway
a hush upon the fleshpots
of Lower Broadway
a pall upon the punk rock
at Mabuhay Gardens
and upon the cafes and bookstores
of old North Beach
a hush upon the landscape
of the still wild West
where two sweet dudes are dead
and no more need be said.
Do not sit upon the ground and speak
of other senseless murderings
or worse disasters waiting
in the wings
Do not sit upon the ground and talk
of the death of things beyond
these sad sad happenings.
Such men as these do rise above
our worst imaginings.

ADIEU À CHARLOT

(Second Populist Manifesto)

Sons of Whitman sons of Poe
sons of Lorca & Rimbaud
or their dark daughters
poets of another breath
poets of another vision
Who among you still speaks of revolution
Who among you still unscrews
the locks from the doors
in this revisionist decade?
'You are President of your own body, America'
Thus spoke Kush in Tepotzlan
youngblood wildhaired angel poet
one of a spawn of wild poets
in the image of Allen Ginsberg
wandering the wilds of America
'You Rimbauds of another breath'
sang Kush
and wandered off with his own particular paranoias
maddened like most poets
for one mad reason or another
in the unmade bed of the world
Sons of Whitman
in your 'public solitude'
bound by blood-duende
'President of your own body America'
Take it back from those who have maddened you
back from those who stole it
and steal it daily
The subjective must take back the world
from the objective gorillas & guerrillas of the world
We must rejoin somehow

the animals in the fields
in their steady-state meditation
'Your life is in your own hands still
Make it flower make it sing'
(so sang mad Kush in Tepotzlan)
'a constitutional congress of the body'
still to be convened to seize control
of the State
the subjective state
from those who have subverted it
The arab telephone of the avant-garde
has broken down
And I speak to you now
from another country
Do not turn away
in your public solitudes
you poets of other visions
of the separate lonesome visions
untamed uncornered visions
fierce recalcitrant visions
you Whitmans of another breath
which is not the too-cool breath of modern poetry
which is not the halitosis of industrial civilization
Listen now Listen again
to the song in the blood the dark duende a dark singing
between the tickings of civilization
between the lines of its headlines
in the silences between cars
driven like weapons
In two hundred years of freedom
we have invented
the permanent alienation of the subjective
almost every truly creative being
alienated & expatriated
in his own country

in Middle America or San Francisco
the death of the dream in your birth
o meltingpot America
I speak to you
from another country
another kind of blood-letting land
from Tepotzlan the poets' lan'
Land of the Lord of the Dawn

                                    Quetzalcoatl

Land of the Plumed Serpent
I signal to you
as Artaud signaled
through the flames
I signal to you
over the heads of the land
the hard heads that stand like menhirs
above the land in every country
the short-haired hyenas
who still rule everything
I signal to you from Poets' Land
you poets of the alienated breath
to take back your land again
and the deep sea of the subjective
Have you heard the sound of the ocean lately
the sound by which daily
the stars still are driven
the sound by which nightly
the stars retake their sky
The sea thunders still to remind you
of the thunder in the blood
to remind you of your selves
Think now of your self
as of a distant ship
Think now of your beloved
of the eyes of your beloved

whoever is most beloved
he who held you hard in the dark
or she who washed her hair by the waterfall
whoever makes the heart pound
the blood pound
Listen says the river
Listen says the sea Within you
you with your private visions
of another reality a separate reality
Listen and study the charts of time
Read the sanskrit of ants in the sand
You Whitmans of another breath
there is no one else to tell
how the alienated generations
have lived out their expatriate visions
here and everywhere
The old generations have lived them out
Lived out the bohemian myth in Greenwich Villages
Lived out the Hemingway myth
in *The Sun Also Rises*
at the Dôme in Paris
or with the bulls at Pamplona
Lived out the Henry Miller myth
in the *Tropics* of Paris
and the great Greek dream
of *The Colossus of Maroussi*
and the tropic dream of Gauguin
Lived out the D. H. Lawrence myth
in *The Plumed Serpent*
in Mexico Lake Chapala
And the Malcolm Lowry myth
Under the Volcano at Cuernavaca
And then the saga of *On the Road*
and the Bob Dylan myth Blowing in the Wind
How many roads must a man walk down

How many Neal Cassadys on lost railroad tracks
How many replicas of Woody Guthrie with cracked guitars
How many photocopies of longhaired Joan
How many Ginsberg facsimiles and carbon-copy Keseys
still wandering the streets of America
in old tennis shoes and backpacks
or driving beat-up school buses
with destination-signs reading 'Further'
How many Buddhist Catholics how many cantors
chanting the Great Paramita Sutra
on the Lower East Side
How many Whole Earth Catalogs
lost in out-houses on New Mexico communes
How many Punk Rockers waving swastikas
Franco is dead but so is Picasso
Chaplin is dead but I'd wear his bowler
having outlived all our myths but his
the myth of the pure subjective
the collective subjective
the Little Man in each of us
waiting with Charlot or Pozzo
On every corner I see them
hidden inside their tight clean clothes
Their hats are not derbys they have no canes
but we know them
we have always
waited with them
They turn and hitch their pants
and walk away from us
down the darkening road
in the great American night

(Tepotzlan '75—San Francisco '78)

LOOK HOMEWARD, JACK:
TWO CORRESPONDENCES

1.

Cruising down long winding highway near Asheville and look-ing East over vast high plain stretched way below Blue Ridge horizon—from high on that highway coming down and round a bend and seeing rapt panorama laid out like the *altoplano* of Tenochtitlan, ancient Aztec Mexico as I saw it coming down past Popocatepetl from the West and Tepotz'lan—the old Aztec capitol there spread out before Cortez under the verdant forest—jungle-like rich deep blue-green woods and fields running to the horizon like some blue-green sea—the whole Aztec civilization alive there hidden under the lush green canopy—a Kerouac vision of the great fellaheen metropole, how it must have looked to a rider coming sudden upon it from the far side of Popo, some great warrior on horseback, stoned on peyotl, with gold head-piece and flashing sword, staring down at the sleeping hidden huge island city in early morn—All gone now, Tenochtitlan buried under.... Mexico City Blues! In the American grain....

2.

In the Thomas Wolfe boardinghouse in Asheville . . . rooms he slept in . . . typewriter he once used . . . his books and clothes and photos . . . one early photo looking exactly like a young Jack Kerouac—set me musing, high on Mexican grass—Sweeping vision of America in *Look Homeward, Angel*, seen by the young Eugene Gant as he rode a train through the American dusk—'to flash upon the window and be gone'—Wolfe's place, said Maxwell Perkins, was all America—So with Jack—Kerouac's vision a car vision, seen from windows of old autos speeding cross-country—the same Wolfian old pre-War America, now all but gone, invisible, except in Greyhound bus stations in small lost towns. . . . And Jack's Lowell, Mass., a mill town and Asheville like a mill town after the mills moved South early in the century, carrying Canuck ghosts with them. . . . Wolfe and Jack drinking together now in eternity . . . omniverous insatiable consumers, of life, which consumed them both too early. . . . Wolfe's stone angel akin to Jack's stone Stations of the Cross in Lowell graveyard, angels of mercy. . . . Both never happy abroad, never happy expatriates—Wolfe drunk in Berlin, Jack stoned on a Mexican rooftop or staggering by the Seine. . . . And which of them would know his brother? . . . Look Homeward, Jack.

FROM 'NORTHWEST ECOLOG'

THE OLD SAILORS

On the green riverbank
                 age late fifties
I am beginning
           to remind myself
of my great Uncle Désir
              in the Virgin Islands
On a Saint Thomas back beach
he lived when I last saw him
in a small shack
             under the palms
Eighty years old
              straight as a Viking
   (where the Danes once landed)
he stood looking out
              over the flat sea
   blue eyes or grey
              with the sea in them
salt upon his lashes
              We
         were always sea wanderers
No salt here now
            by the great river
      in the high desert range
Old sailors stranded
        the steelhead
         they too lost without it
                 leap up and die

WILD LIFE CAMEO, EARLY MORN

By the great river Deschutes
              on the meadowbank greensward
        sun just hitting
                    the high bluffs
          stone cliffs sculpted
                        high away
              across the river

At the foot of a steep brown slope
                          a mile away
            six white-tail deer
          four young bucks with branched antlers
              and two small does
                          mute in eternity
                            drinking the river
        then in real time raising heads
            and climbing up and up
                          a steep faint switchback
                into full sun

I bring them close in the binoculars
                          as in a round cameo
          There is a hollow bole in a tree
                          one looks into
        One by one they
                  drink silence
                          (the two does last)
            one by one
                  climb up so calm
                      over the rim of the canyon
              and without looking back
                          disappear forever

Like certain people
            in my life

CLAMSHELL ALLIANCE

Here by the sea
                    Vashon Island Puget Sound
        at the Portage
                        lie in bed
                            thinking what to do
'The sea
        is calm tonight'
Beneath it
            all not so calm
Nor inside us
                here at this isthmus
        this portage
                    between two lives
        this isthmus
                    built on Indian arrowheads
        all not so calm
We are all
                submerged in our lives
                        in the 'bath of creation'
Yet the tide is full
The small clams and Quilcene oysters
                        are their own alliance
                            against the world's death
They are in league
                with the seas and the whales
They are in league
                with Moby Dick
                    against the Ahabs of earth
The clams
            live and breathe closed up
We too
        close up tight on shore
                                clam up

Yet here by the sea
                    on Vashon
                                        may open out
          in this summerhouse
                                   as in a small Maine seaport
          or wherever—
                              Vashon or Mannahatta—
          the same salt tongue
                              licks us all
The stinging salt
          if we should open up
                                        pours in
          but also the light
                              the lapped light of love. . .
          An illusion by the sea?
                                        a romantic agony?
               a faint flickering
                              in the gloaming?
          At the Coast Guard station
                         the great white lighthouse
                                   still flashes all ways

READING APOLLINAIRE BY THE ROGUE RIVER

Reading Apollinaire here
sitting crosslegged
on sleepingbag & poncho
in the shadow of a huge hill
before the sun clears it
Woke up early on the shore
and heard the river shushing
(like the sound a snake might make
sliding over riprap
if you magnified the sound)
My head still down upon the ground
one eye without perspective
sees the stream sliding by
through the sand
as in a desert landscape
Like a huge green watersnake
with white water markings
the river slithers by
and where the canyon turns
and the river drops from sight
seems like a snake about to disappear
down a deep hole
Indians made their myths
of this great watersnake
slid down from mountains far away
And I see the Rogue for real
as the Indians saw him
the Rogue all wild white water
a cold-blooded creature
drowning and dousing
the Rogue ruler of the land
transforming it at will
with a will of its own

a creature to be feared and respected
pillaging its way to the sea
with great gravity
still ruled by that gravity
which still rules all
so that we might almost say
Gravity is God
manifesting Himself
as Great God Sun
who will one day make Himself
into a black hole in space
who will one day implode Himself
into Nothing
All of which the slithering Rogue
knows nothing of
in its headlong
blind rush to the sea
And though its head
is already being eaten
by that most cruel and churning
monster Ocean
the tail of the snake
knows it not
and continues turning & turning
toward its final hole
and toward that final black hole
into which all some day
will be sucked burning

As I sit reading a French poet
    whose most famous poem is about
        the river that runs through the city
            taking time & life & lovers with it
            And none returning
                    none returning

ROUGH SONG OF ANIMALS DYING

In a dream within a dream I dreamt a dream
of the reality of existence
inside the ultimate computer
which is the universe
in which the Arrow of Time
flies both ways
through bent space
In a dream within a dream I dreamt a dream
of all the animals dying
all animals everywhere
dying & dying
the wild animals the longhaired animals
winged animals feathered animals
clawed & scaled & furry animals
rutting & dying & dying
In a dream within a dream I dreamt a dream
of creatures everywhere dying out
in shrinking rainforests
in piney woods & high sierras
on shrinking prairies & tumbleweed mesas
captured beaten strapped starved & stunned
cornered & traded
species not meant to be nomadic
wandering rootless as man
In a dream within a dream I dreamt a dream
of all the animals crying out
in their hidden places
in the still silent places left to them
slinking away & crawling about
through the last wild places
through the dense underbrush
the last Great Thickets
beyond the mountains

crisscrossed with switchbacks
beyond the marshes
beyond the plains & fences
(the West won with barbed-wire machines)
in the high country
in the low country
crisscrossed with highways
In a dream within a dream I dreamt a dream
of how they feed & rut & run & hide
In a dream within a dream I saw
how the seals are beaten on the ice-fields
the soft white furry seals with eggshell skulls
the Great Green turtles beaten & eaten
exotic birds netted & caged & tethered
rare wild beasts & strange reptiles & weird woozoos
hunted down for zoos
by bearded blackmarketeers
who afterwards ride around Singapore
in German limousines
In a dream within a dream I dreamt a dream
of the earth heating up & drying out
in the famous Greenhouse Effect
under its canopy of carbon dioxide
breathed out by a billion
infernal combustion engines
mixed with the sweet smell of burning flesh
In a dream within a dream I dreamt a dream
of animals calling to each other
in codes we never understand
The seal and steer cry out
in the same voice
as they are clubbed
in Chicago stockyards & Newfoundland snowfields
It is the same cry
The wounds never heal

in the commonweal of animals
We steal their lives
to feed our own
and with their lives
our dreams are sown
In a dream within a dream I dreamt a dream
of the daily scrimmage for existence
in the wind-up model of the universe
the spinning meat-wheel world
in which I was a fish who eats his tail
in which I was a claw upon a beach
in which I was a snake upon a tree
in which I was a serpent's egg
a yin-yang yolk of good and evil
about to consume itself

HORSES AT DAWN

The horses the horses the wild horses at dawn
as in a watercolor by Ben Shahn
they are alive in the high meadow
in the high country on the far mesa
you can see them galloping
you can see them snorting
you can hear their thunder distantly
you can hear the small thunder
of their small hooves
insistently
like wood hammers thrumming
on a distant drum
The sun roars &
throws their shadows
out of the night

CREDITS

"The Old Italians Dying" first was published in the *Los Angeles Times*.

"The Sea and Ourselves at Cape Ann" was printed first in *The New York Times Magazine*, September 11, 1977.

"A Nation of Sheep" appeared in *The New York Times*, May 12, 1979.

"Two Scavengers in a Truck. . ." and "The Billboard Painters" appeared in the *Los Angeles Times*, November 12, 1978, the latter also in the *San Francisco Chronicle and Examiner*, as did "Home Home Home." "White On White," issued as a broadside by the Committee on the Breytenbach Case, also appeared in the *Co-Evolution Quarterly* (Fall 1978).

"Adieu à Charlot" was in the *Los Angeles Times*, March 5, 1978, *San Francisco Examiner*, *City Lights Journal #4*, and *New Directions #38*, and was also printed as broadsides by the Lawton Press (New Rochelle, N.Y.) and White Wail Press (San Francisco). It has been translated and published in France, Germany, and Italy. "An Elegy to Dispel Gloom" came out in the *San Francisco Examiner*, November 29, 1978.

Poems from *Northwest Ecolog* are taken from the City Lights Book (1978).

"Reading Apollinaire by the Rogue River" was first in the *Los Angeles Times*, October 23, 1977.